FREN

Sarah R

FRENCH:
ADVERBS FAST TRACK
LEARNING

The 100 most used French adverbs with 600 phrase examples.

Focus your French learning on the most frequently used adverbs. Learn just the 100 verbs you need for everyday life.

Published by UNITEXTO

FRENCH: ADVERBS FAST TRACK LEARNING
The 100 most used French adverbs

1. Up *Haut*	2. So *Très*	3. Out *A l'extérieur*	4. Just *Juste*
5. Now *Maintenant*	6. How *Comment*	7. Then *Alors*	8. More *Plus*
9. Also *Aussi*	10. Here *Ici*	11. Well *Bien*	12. Only *Seulement*
13. Very *Très*	14. Even *Même*	15. Back *L'arrière*	16. There *Là-bas*
17. Down *En bas*	18. Still *Toujours*	19. In *En*	20. As *Comme*
21. To *Pour*	22. When *Quand*	23. Never *Jamais*	24. Really *Réellement*
25. Most *La plupart*	26. On *Dans*	27. Why *Pourquoi*	28. About *A propos*
29. Over *Terminé*	30. Again *Encore*	31. Where *Où*	32. Right *Droit*
33. Off *Eteint*	34. Always *Toujours*	35. Today *Aujourd'hui*	36. All *Tout*
37. Far *Loin*	38. Long *Long*	39. Away *Loin*	40. Yet *Encore*

41. Often Souvent	42. Ever Jamais	43. However Cependant	44. Almost Presque
45. Later Après	46. Much Beaucoup	47. Once Une fois	48. Least Moins
49. Ago Il y a	50. Together Ensemble	51. Around Autour	52. Already Déjà
53. Enough Assez	54. Both Les deux	55. Maybe Peut-être	56. Actually Francheme nt
57. Probably Probablemen t	58. Home Maison	59. Of Course Bien sûr	60. Perhaps Peut-être
61. Little Petit	62. Else D'autre	63. Sometimes Parfois	64. Finally Finalement
65. Less Moins	66. Better Mieux	67. Early Tôt	68. Especially Spécialeme nt
69. Either Soit	70. Quite Assez	71. Simply Simplement	72. Nearly Quasiment
73. Soon bientôt	74. Certainly Cetrtaineme nt	75. Quickly Rapidement	76. No Pas
77. Recently Récemment	78. Before Avant	79. Usually Souvent	80. Thus Ainsi

81. Exactly *Exactement*	82. Hard *Difficile*	83. Particularly Particulièrement	84. Pretty *Assez*
85. Forward *Avant*	86. Ok *Ok*	87. Clearly Clairement	88. Indeed *En effet*
89. Rather *plutôt*	90. That *Ce*	91. Tonight Ce soir	92. Close *Proche*
93. Suddenly *Soudainement*	94. Best *Meilleur*	95. Instead Au lieu	96. Ahead *Droit*
97. Fast *Rapide*	98. Alone *Seul*	99. Eventually Finalement	100. Directly *Directement*

PHRASE EXAMPLES.
The 100 most used French adverbs

1. Up/*Haut*

He looked *up* and saw the plane	Il a regardé en *haut* et a vu l'avion
The woman went *up* to get a coat	La femme est montée en *haut* pour prendre une couverture
The ballon went *up* with the wind	Le ballon est parti *haut* avec le vent

2. So/T*rès*

She speaks *so* quietly	Elle parle *très* doucement
The movie was *so* boring and stupid	Le film était *très* monotone et stupide
The girl was so nice I couldn't speak	La fille était *très* gentille que je n'ai pas pu parler

3. Out/*à l'extérieur-hors*

This happened *out* of my car	C'est arrivé *à l'extérieur* de ma voiture
I said she couldn't go *out*.	J'ai dit qu'elle ne peut pas sortir *à l'extérieur*
The boat is *out* of sight	Le bateau est *hors* de vu

4. Just/*Juste*

She took *just* what they told her	Elle a pris *juste* ce qu'on lui a demandé
I *just* finished the food	Je viens *juste* de terminer le repas
He is *just* mad, leave him	Il est *juste* fou, laisse-le

5. Now/*Maintenant*

Now I am much older for that	Je suis *maintenant* trop vieux pour ça
I can *now* change the song	Je peux *maintenant* changer la chanson
She knows the truth *now*	Elle connait *maintenant* la vérité

6. How/*Comment-quel*

How are you planning to go?	*Comment* tu prévois d'aller ?
How old is he?	*Quel* âge a-t-il ?
I don´t care *how* you do it	Je me soucie peu *comment* tu l'as fait

7. Then/*Alors-puis*

She was innocent *then*	Elle était innocente *alors*
Then, she changed the subject	*Puis*, elle changé de sujet
Back *then*, we did not do that	*Alors*, nous n'avons pas fait ça

8. More/*Plus*

I want *more* pasta please	Je voudrais *plus* de pattes s'il vous plait
She can have *more* of those	Elle peut avoir *plus* de ceux-là
I don´t care any *more*	Je ne me souci *plus*

9. Also/*aussi*

I *also* got the same color	J'ai aussi eu la même couleur
She could *also* come with you	Elle peut aussi venir avec toi
You can *also* change yours	Tu peux aussi changer le tien

10. Here/*Ici-voici*

You can put it *here*	Tu peux le mettre *ici*
It smells weird in *here*	Ça sent bizarre *ici*
Here is the shoe!	*Voici* les chaussres

11. Well/*Bien*

I feel *well* now, thanks	Je me sens bien maintenant, merci
I treat you *well*, please do the same	Je te traite bien, fais pareil s'il te plait
She is very *well*, bring her	Elle est très bien. Amène-là

12. Only/*Seulement*

I *only* have 12 years of age	J'ai *seulement* 12 ans d'âge
She *only* brought two friends	Elle a *seulement* amené deux amis
Only kids are not allowed	Les enfants *seulement* ne sont pas autorisés

13. Very/*très*

I feel *very* happy about it	Je me sens *très* heureux à ce sujet
She is *very* nice with me	Elle est *très* gentille avec moi
Please be *very* gentle with him	Soyez s'il vous plait *très* gentil avec lui

14. Even/*Même*

Even my mom knows that	*Même* si maman le sait
I *even* brought shoes for that	J'ai *même* acheté des chaussures pour ça
I don't *even* know the truth	Je ne connais *même* pas la vérité

15. Back/*L'arrière*

Look in the *back* of the car	Regarde à l'arrière de la voiture
I don't see anything in the *back*	Je ne vois rien à l'arrière
Can you look *back* on the road?	Pouvez-vous regarder la route à l'arrière ?

16. There/*là-bas*

I saw him *there*, last night	Je l'ai vu *là-bas*
There is my blue shirt	*Là-bas* est ma chemise bleue
She could meet him *there*	Elle peut le rencontrer *là-bas*

17. Down/*en bas*

Put your jacket *down*	Mets ton manteau *en bas*
She was looking *down* all day	Elle regardait *en bas* toute la journée
I can´t take you *down* there	Je ne peux pas t'emmener *en bas*

18. Still/*Toujours*

There is *still* hope for that	Il y a *toujours* un espoir pour ça
I *still* know that	Je sais *toujours* ça
She could *still* be my friend	Elle pourrait *toujours* être mon amie

19. In/ *Dans*

She saw *in* the movie that style	Elle a vu *dans* le film ce style
I looked *in* the room	J'ai regardé *dans* la chambre

11

In my house we have pasta	*Dans* ma maison nous avons des pattes

20. As/*Comme*

She introduced me *as* her friend	Elle m'a présenté *comme* un ami
As you might know we got divorced	*Comme* vous le savez, nous avons divorcé
It is *as* long as my hair	C'est long *comme* mes cheuveux

21. To/*Pour*

I brought this *to* play	J'ai apporté ça *pour* jouer
To have this, I saved a lot	*Pour* avoir ceci, j'ai beaucoup epargné
To change her style you need this	*Pour* changer son style vous avez besoin de ça

22. When/*Quand*

When are you coming home?	Quand viendrez-vous à la maison ?
This was *when* she brought my car	C'était quand elle a apporté ma voiture
When you will be ready?	Quand serez-vous prêts ?

23. Never/*Jamais*

You should *never* paint	Vous ne devez *jamais*

those walls	peindre ces murs
I *never* thought I could see you	Je ne pensais *jamais* que je vous verrai
You *never* bring them along	Ne les amenez *jamais* avec vous

24. Really/*Vraiment*

I *really* thought we could change	Je pensais *vraiment* que nous pourrions changer
She *really* doesn´t know me	Elle ne me connait pas *vraiment*
We *really* like that shirt	Nous aimons *vraiment* cette chemise

25. Most/*La plupart*

Most of the people came late	*La plupart* des gens arrivent en retard
I told *most* of them to come	J'ai dit à *la plupart* d'entre eux de venir
Most of the houses are green	*La plupart* des maisons sont verts

26. On/*Dans-allumé-sur*

On my birthday I will sing	*Dans* mon anniversaire, je vais chanter
I left the radio *on*.	J'ai laissé la radio *allumée*
She left it *on* the table.	Elle l'a laissé *sur* la table

27. Why/*Pourquoi*

Why would you change that?	Pourquoi changeriez-vous cela ?
I asked her why she did it	Je lui ai demandé pourquoi elle l'a fait
Why are you coming late?	Pourquoi venez-vous en retard ?

28. About/à propos

This is about a little dog	C'est à propos d'un petit chien
I will talk about it later	Je parlerai à propos de ça après
She came to talk about my cat	Elle est venue parler à propos de mon chat

29. Over/terminé-sur

I told him the party was over	Je lui ai dit que la fête est terminée
I placed it over the table	Je l'ai placé sur la table
The concert was over earlier	Le concert s'est terminé plus tôt

30. Again/encore

I won't do that again	Je ne le ferai pas encore
Again, we can see the movie	Encore, nous pouvons regardé le film
I want to go there again	Je veux aller là-bas encore

31. Where/*Où*

Where would you like to be?	*Où* voudriez-vous être ?
Where the dreams come true	*Où* les rêves deviennent réalité
I asked *where* I could park	J'ai demandé *où* est ce que je pourrais stationner

32. Right/*Droit-Avoir raison*

I have the *right* to know about it	J'ai le *droit* de le savoir
I know she was *right*	Je sais qu'elle avait *raison*
I left it in the *right* corner	Je l'ai laissé dans le coin *droit*

33. Off/E*teindre*

This couldn't be turned *off*	On ne peut pas l'*éteindre*
I had to turn the TV *off* last night	J'ai dû *éteindre* la télé hier soir
The stove was *off* yesterday	Le four était *éteint* hier

34. Always/T*oujours*

I *always* knew she was fine	J'ai *toujours* su qu'elle allait bien
Always bring comfortable shoes	apportez *Toujours* des chaussures confortables
I *always* sing in the car	Je chante *toujours* dans la

	voiture

35. Today/*Aujourd'hui*

I need to finish *today*	Je dois finir a*ujourd'hui*
Today is a great day	*Aujourd'hui* est un beau jour
I can't have it by *today*	Je ne peux pas l'avoir a*ujourd'hui*

36. All/*tout*

All of the above is a lie	*Tout* ce qu'il y a en dessous est un mensonge
All the world is about to end	*Tout* le monde est en train de finir
I have brough *all* the water	J'ai apporté *toute* l'eau

37. Far/*Loin*

I live *far* away	J'habite *loin* d'ici
I can't go that *far* like this	Je ne peux aller aussi *loin* comme ça
She said it was not *far* away	Elle a dit que ce n'était pas *loin*

38. Long/*Long*

This was a *long* day	C'était une *longue* journée
I love her new *long* dress	J'aime sa nouvelle *longue*

	robe
It is 32 inches *long*	Il fait 32 pouces de *long*

39. Away/*Absent*

I was *away* for that holiday	J'étais *absent* pendant ces vacances
Please go *away*	*Va-t'en* s'il te plait
She planned to be *away* this time	Elle a prévu d'être *absente* cette fois

40. Yet/*Encore*

I can't find the right dress *yet*	Je ne peux pas trouver la bonne robe *encore*
We can't disclose the image *yet*	Nous ne pouvons pas dévoiler l'image *encore*
I don't know *yet*, it's a surprise	Je ne sais pas *encore*, c'est une surprise

41. Often/*Souvent*

We think of you *often*	Nous pensons *souvent* à vous
I *often* drink this pills	Je prends *souvent* ces pilules
I am *often* away from the house	Je suis *souvent* absent de la maison

42. Ever/*Jamais*

Nothing *ever* seemed to kill her	*Jamais* rien ne semble la tuer
Nothing *ever* changes	*Jamais* rien ne change
No one will *ever* experience that	*Jamais* personne ne vivra ça

43. However/*Cependant*

However, we can´t do those changes	*Cependant*, nous ne pouvons pas faire ces changements
It may, *however* be recognized	Ça se peut, *cependant* être reconnu
I can´t, *however*, she maybe can	Je ne peux pas, *cependant*, elle peut

44. Almost/Presque

Almost always I can jump	*Presque* toujours je peux sauter
Almost everyone knows her	*Presque* tout le monde la connait
I *almost* fell off the plane	Je suis *presque* tombé de l'avion

45. Later/*après*

I can talk to you *later*	Je peux te parler *après*
She will come *later*, don´t worry	Elle viendra *après*, ne vous inquiétez pas
I´ll drink them *later*	Je les boirai *après*

46. Much/*Beaucoup-combien*

I don't think of him *much*	Je ne pense pas *beaucoup* à lui
I know how *much* you worked	Je sais *combien* tu as travaillé
She didn't make *much* noise	Elle n'a pas fait *beaucoup* de bruit

47. Once/*Une fois*

Once I met her	*Une fois* je l'ai rencontré
I can't take them all at *once*	Je ne peux pas les prendre tous *à la fois*
I knocked the door *once*	J'ai frappé à la porte *une fois*

48. Least/*Moins*

At *least* bring her upstairs	*Au moins* emmène-là en haut
At *least* she sang 2 songs	*Au moins* elle chanté 2 chansons
Make it at *least* 2mts. long	Fais-le *au moins* 2 mètres long

49. Ago/*il y a*

I changed that 2 days *ago*	J'ai changé ça *il y a* 2 jours
That was centuries *ago*	C'était *il y a* des siècles

A long time *ago*, I changed this	*Il y a* longtemps, j'ai changé ça

50. Together/*Ensemble*

Together we can make this better	*Ensemble* nous pouvons le rendre mieux
Everyone *together* looks better	Tout le monde *ensemble* parait mieux
They are *together* since 1975	Ils sont *ensemble* depuis 1975

51. Around/*Autour*

I have been *around* this house already	J'ai déjà été autour de cette maison
I don't play *around* here	Je ne joue pas autour d'ici
Draw a circle *around* de the stone	Dessine un cercle autour du rocher

52. Already/*déjà*

I have *already* met the goal	J'ai *déjà* atteint le but
You know me *already*	Vous me connaissez *déjà*
I *already* gave up on that dream	J'ai *déjà* renoncé à ce rêve

53. Enough/*Assez*

I don't know her well	Je ne la connais *assez* bien

enough	
I know when it is *enough*	Je sais quand c'est *assez*
I can't thank you *enough*	Je ne peux pas vous remercier *assez*

54. Both/*Deux*

Both are red colored	Les *deux* sont rouges
Both my kids are 17	Mes *deux* enfants ont 17ans
I bought them *both* to be sure	J'ai acheté les *deux* pour être sûr

55. Maybe/*Peut-être*

Maybe you should call her	Vous devrez *peut-être* l'appeler
I can *maybe* bring two of those	Je peux *peut-être* apporter deux de ceux-là
Can you *maybe* say it again?	Pouvez-vous *peut-être* le redire ?

56. Actually/*Franchement*

Actually I don't need a car	*Franchement*, je n'ai pas besoin d'une voiture
I don't *actually* remember her name	*Franchement* je ne me souviens de son nom
I think you could *actually* bring it	Je crois que vous devriez *franchement* l'apporter

57. Probably/*Probablement*

Probably she is not in the list	*Probablement* elle n'est pas sur la liste
I am *probably* too late	Je suis *probablement* en retard
I can *probably* fix that	Je peux *probablement* réparer ça

58. Home/*Maison*

My *home* is where my heart is	Ma *maison* est là où est mon cœur
This is Maria´s *home*	C'est la *maison* de Maria
I feel like *home*	Je me sens comme à la *maison*

59. Of Course/*Bien sûr*

Of course you can come with me	*Bien sûr* que vous pouvez m'accompagner
I can *of course* offer you a discount	Je peux *bien sûr* vous offrir une réduction
Of course I won´t leave you here	*Bien sûr* je ne vous laisserai pas ici

60. Perhaps/*Peut-être*

Perhaps you need something like it	Vous avez *peut-être* besoin de quelque chose comme ça
Perhaps she´ll come too	Elle viendra aussi *peut-*

	être
We can *perhaps* improve it	Nous pouvons *peut-être* l'améliorer

61. Little/*Petit*

This *little* horse is mine	Ce *petit* cheval est le mien
I have a *Little* friend at home	J'ai un *petit* copain à la maison
This is too *Little* for me	C'est trop *petit* pour moi

62. Else/*Sinon-d'autre*

You can come, or *else* stay here	Tu peux venir, *sinon* reste ici
Ask that to someone *else*	Demande à quelqu'un *d'autre*
I will go, or *else* I will regret it	Je vais partir, *sinon* je vais le regretter

63. Sometimes/*Parfois*

Sometimes I wonder how it goes	*Parfois* je me demande comment ça marche
I can *sometimes* come at 8:00	Je peux *parfois* venir à 8 :00
Can you *sometimes* call me?	Peux-tu m'appeler *parfois* ?

64. Finally/*finalement*

I can *finally* say I graduated	Je peux *finalement* dire que j'ai mon diplôme
Finally, just add the eggs	*Finalement*, ajoutez seulement les œufs
I can *finally* ask her that	Je peux *finalement* lui demander ça

65. Less/Moins

Wear something *less* revealing	Porte quelque chose de *moins* révélateur
I have much *less* than you do.	J'ai beaucoup *moins* que ce que vous avez
I couldn't care *less* about it	Je ne peux pas me soucier *moins* de ça

66. Better/*Mieux*

I feel a lot *better* now	Je me sens beaucoup *mieux* maintenant
I can fix that *better* than you do	Je peux le réparer *mieux* que toi
This is to keep it in a *better* place	Ceci est pour *mieux* le placer

67. Early/*Temprano*

I woke up really *early* today	Je me suis réveillé vraiment *tôt* aujourd'hui
I can say that, it's too *early*	Je ne peux pas dire ça, c'est trop *tôt*

This was an *early* call	C'est un appel *tôt* le matin

68. Especially/*Spécialement*

Especially if you don't like it	*Spécialement* si vous ne l'aimez pas
I bought it *especially* for you	Je l'ai acheté *spécialement* pour toi
This is *especially* made by me	C'est fait *spécialement* par moi

69. Either/*Soit*

Either you come or you go	*Soit* vous venez ou vous partez
Either 10 or 20 is a good price	*Soit* 10 ou 20 est un bon prix
I can *either* choose green or red	Je peux *soit* choisir le vert ou le rouge

70. Quite/*Assez-quelques*

That was *quite* enough	C'était *assez*
I have *quite* some friends	J'ai *quelques* amis
I don't have *quite* enough food	Je n'ai pas *assez* de nourriture

71. Simply/*Simplement*

I can *simply* change it	Je peux *simplement* le changer

This is *simply* the best trip	C'est *simplement* le meilleur voyage
I don't *simply* use it like that	Je ne l'utilise pas *simplement* comme ça

72. Nearly/*Quasiment*

I *nearly* lose you	Je t'ai *quasiment* perdu
I *nearly* miss the train	J'ai *quasiment* raté le train
This was *nearly* a bad experience	C'était *quasiment* une mauvaise expérience

73. Soon/*Bientôt-dès*

She will come *soon*, Hurry!	Elle viendra *bientôt*, fais vite
I will *soon* know if she is coming	Je saurai *bientôt* si elle va venir
I can change it as *soon* as you go	Je peux le changer *dès* que vous partez

74. Certainly/*Certainement*

Certainly that is a bad word	*Certainement* c'est un mauvais mot
I can *certainly* assure it won't happen	Je peux *certainement* assurer que ça n'arrivera pas
Certainly Harry lost the game	*Certainement* Harry a perdu le jeu

75. Quickly/Vite-*Rapidement*

Quickly! Change it now!	*Vite* ! Change le maintenant
I can *quickly* change my mind	Je peux *rapidement* changer d'avis
This was done *quickly*	Ça a été fait *rapidement*

76. No/*Pas*

I have *no* shoes for tonight	Je n'ai *pas* de chaussures pour ce soir
There is *no* people here	Il n'y a *pas* de gens ici
I will have *no* memory by then	Je n'aurai *pas* de mémoire d'ici-là

77. Recently/*Récemment*

This was done *recently*	Ça a été fait *récemment*
I *recently* quit my job	J'ai *récemment* quitté mon travail
She *recently* got surgery too	Elle a *récemment* eu une opération aussi

78. Before/*Avant*

I knew this *before* you	J'ai su ça *avant* toi
Before, this was not a problem	*Avant*, ce n'était pas un problème
I can go there *before* your house	Je peux aller là-bas *avant* ta maison

79. Usually/*Souvent*

I *usually* don´t change those	Je ne les change pas *souvent*
She *usually* wears blouses	Elle porte *souvent* des chemises
This *usually* doesn´t happen	Ça n'arrive pas *souvent*

80. Thus/*Ainsi*

I will go, *thus* she will have no option	J'irai, *ainsi* elle n'aura pas le choix
Thus, it was fortified with light	*Ainsi*, ça a été fortifié avec la lumière
Thus the honor would be divided	*Ainsi*, l'honneur serait divisé

81. Exactly/*Exactement*

I know *exactly* where that is	Je sais *exactement* où c'est
She did *exactly* the same	Elle a fait *exactement* la même chose
This went *exactly* as planned	Ça s'est passé *exactement* comme prévu

82. Hard/*Difficile*

This was a *hard* choice	C'est un choix *difficile*
This is as *hard* as it can get	C'est aussi *difficile* que possible

I know how *hard* it is	Je sais combien c'est *difficile*

83. Particularly/*Particilièrement*

I *particularly* don't care about it	Je ne me soucie *particulièrement* de rien
I don't *particularly* look for these	Je ne recherché pas *particulièrement* ceux-là
She will *particularly* point them out	Elle va *particulièrement* les désigner

84. Pretty/*Joli-Assez*

She looks *pretty* in that dress	Elle est *jolie* dans cette robe
That was a *pretty* fun ride	C'est un tour *assez* amusant
This was *pretty* funny, thanks!	C'était *assez* amusant, merci !

85. Forward/*Avant*

Move the table *forward* to see it	Bouge la table en *avant* pour le voir
I can't move *forward* anymore	Je ne peux plus bouger en *avant*
She kept looking *forward*	Elle continua de regarder à *l'avant*

86. Ok/*Ok*

She will be *ok* with that	Elle sera *ok* avec ça
I don't think you are *ok*	Je ne crois pas que t'es *ok*
She was *ok* with that decision	Elle était *ok* avec cette décision

87. Clearly/*Clairement*

Clearly, this wasn't clever	*Clairement*, ce n'était pas malin
We *clearly*, don't know what it is	Nous ne savons *clairement* pas ce que c'est
I couldn't see *clearly*	Je ne pouvais pas voir *clairement*

88. Indeed/*En effet*

Indeed it is a good deal	*En effet*, c'est une bonne affaire
I can *indeed* change it for you	Je peux *en effet* le changer pour vous
I will *indeed* ask for it	Je vais *en effet* le demander

89. Rather/*Plutôt-préfère*

I *rather* choose the green	Je choisis *plutôt* le vert
I *rather* not know about it	Je *préfère* ne pas le savoir
I *rather* eat sushi for dinner	Je *préfère* manger du sushi au diner

90. That/*C'-ce*

30

That is not how I imagined it	*Ce* n'est pas comme je l'ai imagine
I can't tell if *that* is it	Je ne peux pas dire si *c'*est ça
That is what I wanted	*C'*est ce que je voulais

91. Tonight/*Ce soir*

Tonight we will finally see it	*Ce soir* ne le verrons enfin
I will have it by *tonight*	Je l'aurai *ce soir*
I can't change it until *tonight*	Je ne peux pas le changer jusqu'à *ce soir*

92. Close/Proche-*Fermer*

That was pretty *close* to me	C'était assez *proche* pour moi
I can *close* the door for this	Je peux *fermer* la porte pour ça
I can't be too *close* to you	Je ne peux pas être plus *proche* de toi

93. Suddenly/*Soudainement*

Suddenly, this all changed my mind	*Soudainement*, tout ça me fit changer d'avis
I *suddenly* realized the truth	J'ai *soudainement* réalisé la vérité
I *suddenly* reacted to that	J'ai réagi *soudainement* à ça

31

94. Best/Meilleur

That was the *best* deal	C'était la *meilleure* affaire
You are my *best* friend	Tu es mon *meilleur* ami
I don't know the *best* place	Je ne connais pas la *meilleure* place

95. Instead/*Au lieu*

Instead of cleaning, I'll sllep	*Au lieu de nettoyer, je vais dormir*
Instead of turning, ill go straight	*Au lieu de tourner, j'irai droit*
I chose you *instead* of her	Je t'ai choisi au lieu d'elle

96. Ahead/*Droit-attendre*

I'll go *ahead* and do it	J'irai *droit* et le ferai
I know there is work *ahead*	Je sais qu'il y a du travail qui nous *attend*
She is *ahead* of us here	Elle nous *attend* ici

97. Fast/*Rapide*

That was a *fast* meal	C'était un repas *rapide*
I can't change it that *fast*	Je ne peux pas le changer aussi *rapidement*
I know that was very *fast*	Je sais que c'était très *rapide*

98. Alone/*Seul*

I will leave him *alone* now	Je le laisserai *seul* maintenant
I can´t be *alone* all the time	Je ne peux pas être *seul* tout le temps
I know you want to be *alone*	Je sais que tu veux rester *seul*

99. Eventually/*finalement*

Eventually you´ll find a job	*Finalement,* tu vas trouver un travail
I know *eventually* she´ll come	Je sais qu'elle viendra *finalement*
She is *eventually* moving out	Elle va *finalement* déménager

100.   Directly/*Directement*

I know who to contact *directly*	Je sais qui contacter *directement*
She is *directly* related to me	Elle est *directement* reliée à moi
I lied *directly* to his face	J'ai menti *directement* à son visage

THE END

Printed in Great Britain
by Amazon